TRIPLE
SNAPS

ALSO BY 2 BROS. & A WHITE GUY, INC.: *SNAPS* AND *DOUBLE SNAPS*

TRIPLE
SNAPS

JAMES PERCELAY, MONTERIA IVEY, AND STEPHAN DWECK

 **BROS. & A WHITE GUY, INC.**

FOREWORD BY ICE-T

PHOTOGRAPHS BY KWAKU ALSTON

QUILL
WILLIAM MORROW
NEW YORK

4

Library of Congress Cataloging-in-Publication Data

Percelay, James.
  Triple snaps / James Percelay, Monteria Ivey, Stephan Dweck; foreword by Ice-T.—1st ed.
    p. cm.
  ISBN 0-688-14591-4
  1. Afro-Americans—Language (new words, slang, etc.).
2. English language—United States—Terms and phrases.
3. Afro-American wit and humor. 4. Afro-Americans—quotations. 5. Quotations, American. 6. Black English.
7. Americanisms. 8. Invective. I. Ivey, Monteria. II. Dweck, Stephan. III. Title.
PE3727.N4P48 1995
427'.973'08996—dc20   95-42854
                                                 CIP

Printed in the United States of America

First Edition

1 2 3 4 5 6 7 8 9 10

PHOTOGRAPHS BY KWAKU ALSTON
BOOK DESIGN BY ELIZABETH VAN ITALLIE

To my parents, Merrill and Sheela;
twin brother, Bruce Andrew; brother David; Noreen; and Aunt Phyllis.
—JAMES L. PERCELAY

To my family, friends, and fans,
who have made the Snaps journey a labor of love.
—MONTERIA IVEY

To the "crown jewel," Lisa Victoria Chapman Jones.
—STEPHAN DWECK

CONTRIBUTING EDITOR
Michelle Cuccini

ᶜ

ADDITIONAL SNAPS WRITTEN BY
(in alphabetical order) Capital J, Randy Fechter, Uncle Jimmy Mack,
The Most Brothers, Sam Silver, Will Sylvince

THE DARK SNAPPER illustrated by Hype Comics

TRIPLE THANKS to our editor, **WILL SCHWALBE**

SPECIAL THANKS TO
Roger Burlage, Paul Almond, Yalda Teheranian, and the
talented people at Live Entertainment; Cella Irvine, Donna Campbell,
Bob Risse, Kevin Labick, and the wired team at Hearst New Media;
the hip crew at Atlantic Records/Big Beat Records;
Michael Rosenfeld Gallery

WE APPRECIATE THE SUPPORT OF THESE PEOPLE
Gary Sharfin; Janice Young; Chester Mapp; Fig; Doris Cooper;
Vince Anelle; Sonya McLaughlin; our attorney, Michael Rudell; and our
agents, Mary Evans and Ron Bernstein

FOREWORD
BY ICE-T

I THINK SNAPPING is the national pastime for black youth in America. In many ways the game is a form of male bonding. It's a statement of friendship that I don't think has ever been explained. You can't play this game with your enemies. With your boy you can hit him in the chest or wrestle on the ground and everything is cool. The same with snapping. I can talk crazy and jump all over you when we're snapping because of the closeness.

When I was growing up we called it playing the dozens or baggin'. Then there were the guys who liked to free-style. They start out with stuff like "You big, greasy, chicken-eatin', two-liter-Pepsi drinking . . . " and they go on and on with all kinds of ill shit made up just from looking at you. It isn't really a joke, but it's funny as hell. Free-style.

I could get off, but I've known some guys who were great. King T and I used to share an apartment and we had a friend named Ant. Ant would sit up all night with King T and the Alcoholics and they would just go at it, nonstop. I used to tell Ant that he should become a professional and get paid, because he was one crazy motherfucker. Now he's a comedian by the name of A. J. Johnson and he was in the movie *Panther.* Biz Markie is good too. I once shared a tour bus with Biz and we had a lot of fun.

I know some people get offended by snapping. Say one thing to them and they ain't with it. All they can do is just look your way and say, "Well . . . fuck you." I've got a friend that I do my music with, and this guy can't take a joke. I told him, "Look, we talk shit because we're friends." Some people are just too sensitive, while others try to overintellectualize shit. They want to make everything sane in an insane world.

I think hip-hop is the best thing ever to happen in this country, and I see a connection between all the attention that snapping has been getting and the emergence of the hip-hop nation. In fact, I can put it in one simple word . . . real. Hip-hop is a whole culture based on "How do you really feel? What's the real deal about the 'hood?" Hip-hop represents a healthy rebellion against the status quo, and snapping is a part of that. Snapping is real. It's what we do. It's about being able to bathe ourselves in our own humility by making fun of how fucked up shit is. It's funny when you say, "Your house was so dirty the rats wore snowshoes." But at the same time I can imagine the joke being true because maybe my house was kind of messed up once. So the game comes from a place of truth, and that's what makes me laugh. Being real also means having dimension. One minute I can be as serious as a heart attack, and the next I could be snapping on your head. The other thing snapping and hip-hop have in common is that they will never go away. They are here to stay.

I know some women get offended by the game. Sometimes I think women get offended by everything. I understand. I try to deal with the whole male-female issue in my music. But when you get down to cases, I know some women who are among the best snappers out there. Some women can roll with the punches better than men. I know some women who are harder, have dirtier mouths, and will kill you quicker than a man. Sometimes I might be able to kick it with my girl and we can snap on each other, but I don't want her snapping on me out in public. Snapping is like anything else in life, cool for some but not for others.

I don't agree with the people who think that snapping has gone main-stream and is selling out. Selling out is when you do something that runs counter to your integrity and your heart. There is nothing wrong with being successful and having fun at the same time. It's about time black people got paid for something we created before some-body else comes along, claims it, and makes a movie with Leslie Nielsen snapping. Why should we be on the sidelines while somebody else gets the glory talking about "Oh . . . you know . . . we invented that . . . "? Selling out. People throw that term around like crazy.

Let's talk about the black people who want to distance themselves from anything "too black" and who think snapping is like our dirty laundry that we shouldn't air in public. Now that's the sellout. You have to remember that the sellout is available when you start to care too much about material bullshit, which is really only on loan. Anybody who is concerned about dirty laundry needs to realize that all that means is that you are too worried about what white people think about you. You'll never make them happy, because you will always be black. If this is what we do, then this is what we do, and if you don't like it you can kiss our ass. It is important that black folks learn to be happy about being black. The bottom line is that there are a lot of people who wish they could do this, but they can't. Meanwhile, we're sitting around wondering what do they think of us.

Too many older people think just because white people aren't whipping us, we should just be quiet Toms. If you say "Kiss my ass" right up front, they'll leave you alone. Then, instead of being a sellout, you'll be "that crazy n—." We should enjoy snapping. It comes out of the culture. If black people can't enjoy who we are, the good and the bad, then we are the ones who are really missing out.

PEACE.

CONTENTS

SNAPPING RULES

1. Don't touch your opponent.

2. Use a referee.

3. Snap in front of a crowd.

4. Don't spit.

FAT
SNAPS

Your sister is so fat, every time she goes to a barbecue they put an apple in her mouth.

Your mother is so fat, **HER BUTT HAS MORE BASS** than a car speaker.

Your mother is so fat, her maiden name was Bacon.

Your mother is so fat, when she farted with jeans on it looked like a mouse ran down her leg.

Your mother is so fat, when she has sex guys ask for directions.

Your mother is so fat, she has to douche with a Super Soaker.

Your father is so fat, when he farts smoke alarms go off.

Your mother is so fat, she **EATS HER CEREAL** out of a satellite dish.

You're mother is so fat, she stepped onto a talking elevator and it said, "I'm falling and I can't get up!"

YOUR MOTHER IS SO FAT, she walked on a bridge and it collapsed.

Your girlfriend is so fat, when I got on top of her I burned my ass **ON THE LIGHT BULB.**

Your mother's ass is so big, when she farts it sounds like a round of applause.

Your mother is so fat, she can't board a bus without blowing the tires.

Your mother is so fat, her mailbox says **HOME OF THE WHOPPER.**

Your sister is so fat, she can use a circus tent for a miniskirt.

Your mother is so fat, she puts on lipstick with a paint roller.

Your mother is so fat, the highway patrol made her wear a sign saying CAUTION! WIDE LOAD.

Your mother is so fat, when she auditioned for a part in *Raiders of the Lost Ark* she got cast as the rolling boulder.

Your mother is so fat, when she stands up the sun goes down.

Your mother is so fat, when she went to Texas the cowboys tried to round her up and brand her.

Your mother is so fat, when she steps into the ocean it becomes high tide.

Your sister is so fat, **HER BUTT LOOKS LIKE TWO PIGS** fighting over a Milk Dud.

Your mother is so fat, when she rides the bus they charge her double fare.

Your brother is so fat, when he walks by I feel an aftershock.

Your mother is so fat, she **SHITS CRISCO.**

YOUR MOTHER IS SO FAT, HER UNDER-WEAR HAS MUDFLAPS.

You're so fat, **WHEN YOU WALK DOWN THE STREET** there is no other side.

You're so fat, the only time you see *90210* is on the scale.

Your mother's legs are so fat, when she walks it looks like she's just gliding across the floor.

Your mother is so fat, she couldn't **FLOAT IN SPACE.**

Your mother is so fat, she put on a black dress and everybody yelled, "Shamu."

Your mother is so fat, her yearbook picture WAS AN AERIAL PHOTO.

Your mother is so fat, she carpools by herself.

Your mother is so fat, when she plays hopscotch she goes "L.A., Chicago, New York, Paris."

Your mother is so fat, when she bungee-jumped SHE WENT STRAIGHT TO HELL.

Your mother is so fat, her double chin looks like my ass.

Your sister is so fat, when she tried computer dating it matched her up with Detroit.

Your mother is so fat, SHE COULD MOON EUROPE.

Your mother is so fat, mosquitoes see her and scream, "Buffet!"

Your father is so fat, he goes to a restaurant, looks at a menu, and says, "Okay."

Your mother is so fat, when she eats at McDonald's you can watch the numbers change.

Your mother is so fat, she stood in front of the **HOLLYWOOD** sign and it read **HD**.

Your mother is so fat, she thinks gravy is a beverage.

Your mother is so fat, she eats Wheat Thicks.

Your mother is so fat, she has her own brand of jeans, FA—Fat Ass jeans.

Your mother is so fat, the weather service gives **NAMES TO HER FARTS.**

Your mother is so fat, **SHE THINKS LITE FOOD** means under a ton.

Your brother is so fat, his motorcycle has two side cars—one for each butt cheek.

Your mother is so fat, **SHE FELL IN LOVE AND BROKE IT.**

Your face is so fat, a crane couldn't give you a face lift.

Your mother is so fat, she uses a big screen for a Watchman.

Your sister is so fat, when she walks down the street **CAR ALARMS GO OFF.**

You're sister is so fat, she can't wear One Size Fits All.

Your girlfriend is so fat, when she sits on my face I can't hear the stereo.

Your mother is so fat, Goodyear rents her out for the Super Bowl.

YOUR MOTHER EATS SO MUCH, she gets more runs than a pair of stockings.

YOUR MOTHER IS SO FAT, IF SHE BENT OVER THEY COULD SHOW A DOUBLE FEATURE ON HER ASS.

You're so fat, your clothes don't have wire hangers, they have **AIRPLANE HANGARS.**

Your mother is so fat, she's not on Slim Fast, she's on Slim Chance.

Your mother is so fat, she gets her own weather reports.

You're so fat, you have Dick Do syndrome, 'cause your belly hangs out more than your dick do.

You're so fat, **EVERY TIME YOU PUT ON NIKES** they spell Nickelodeon.

Your mother is so fat, when she was born they baptized her in tartar sauce.

Your father is so fat, HIS DICK HAS ROLLS.

Your father is so fat, when he was a kid he ate his chicken pox.

You're so fat, when your landlord looked at you he doubled THE RENT.

Your mother is so fat, she went on a fourteen-day diet and the only thing she lost was two weeks.

STUPID

SNAPS

Your sister is so stupid, she tried to get a job picking cotton candy.

Your mother is so stupid, she told me to meet her at the corner of WALK AND DON'T WALK.

Your brother is so stupid, when his girlfriend told him to do it doggy style he lay down in the driveway and licked his balls.

Your mother is so stupid, she thought A DINOSAUR was a venereal disease.

Your sister is so stupid, she went to The Gap to get her teeth fixed.

Your mother is so country, she likes hog calling because it's **DINNER AND A DATE.**

Your mother is so stupid, she thinks a two-income family is when your daddy has two jobs.

Your sister is so stupid, when she missed her period she checked **THE LOST AND FOUND.**

Your father is so stupid, he thought misunderstanding was a woman.

Your father is so stupid, he took a fishing pole to Sea World.

Your mother is so stupid, she thought she had to be dead to eat SOUL FOOD.

Your mother is so stupid, she thought eat and run was an Olympic event.

Your brother is so stupid, he poured water on his pillow to get a wet dream.

Your mother is so dumb, SHE ATE YEAST because she wanted to rise early.

Your father is so stupid, he thought fruit punch was a gay boxer.

Your mother is so stupid, she doesn't use toothpaste because **NONE OF HER TEETH ARE LOOSE.**

Your sister is so stupid, every time she gets an Oscar Mayer wiener she gives an acceptance speech.

Your mother is so stupid, she wants to be a cross between a ho and a computer so she can be a fuckin' know-it-all.

Your mother is so stupid, she thought **DEATH ROW** was the best seats at a funeral.

Your mother is so stupid, she thinks hummingbirds hum because they forgot the words.

Your mother is so stupid, she says she can't play water polo because she can't find a horse that swims.

Your brother is so stupid, he put himself in **A HEAD LOCK** so no one could steal his thoughts.

Your father is so stupid, when I told him to take the garbage out, he asked, "Is it Mother's Day already?"

Your mother is so stupid, every time she blinks she gets lost.

Your mother is so stupid, there was a sign that said **FINE FOR PARKING,** so she parked.

Your mother is so stupid, she went to the drugstore for K-Y jelly because she didn't want the meat to stick.

Your mother is so stupid, she eats jellyfish with peanut butter.

Your mother is so stupid, she thought an **AUTOBIOGRAPHY** was a book on cars.

Your mother is so stupid, she thought Sister Sledge was a nun.

Your sister is so stupid, she got on *Soul Train* and asked if it went local or express.

Your mother is so stupid, when I said I was gonna take the day off she asked, "When you gonna PUT IT BACK?"

Your mother is such a stupid drunk, she became a lawyer to join the Bar.

Your mother is so stupid, she thinks Snoop Doggy Dogg kicks it with Charlie Brown.

Your mother is so stupid, she watches *The Three Stooges* and takes notes.

You're so stupid, you think homophobia is the fear of going home.

Your father is so stupid, he thought Manual Labor was THE PRESIDENT OF MEXICO.

You're so stupid, you think Sir-Mix-a-Lot is good with vodka.

Your mother is so stupid, she thinks CDs are located between B and E at the music store.

Your sister is so stupid, she thought the way to have twins was to **HAVE SEX WHEN YOU'RE PREGNANT.**

Your sister is so stupid, she thought Summer's Eve was the night before summer starts.

Your father is so stupid, he thought LL Cool J was an air conditioner.

Your father is so stupid, he invented an inflatable dart board.

Your sister is so stupid, when she gets sick **SHE DRINKS DR PEPPER.**

Your mother is so stupid, she tried to commit suicide by jumping out of the basement window.

Your father is so stupid, he thinks Grape-Nuts is an STD.

Your mother is so stupid, **SHE CALLS BEEPERS** collect.

Your father is so dumb, he bought an elephant instead of a car because it had a bigger trunk.

Your mother is so stupid, I told her she stepped in manure and she said, "No Shit!"

Your mother is so dumb, she put sugar on her pillow because she wanted to have **SWEET DREAMS.**

Your sister is so stupid, she thought a werewolf was an animal that was never around.

Your brother is so stupid, he lost his job as an elevator operator 'cause he couldn't remember the route.

Your mother is so stupid, she got caught cheating on her blood test.

Your mother is so stupid, she thought Popeyes was an eye clinic.

Your sister is so stupid, when I told her to give me a ring she went to the **JEWELRY STORE.**

Your mother is so stupid, I told her a train was coming and she said, "Okay, as long as it doesn't come in my mouth."

Your mother is so stupid, she thought an IOU was a college.

You're so stupid, when the cashier asked you if you were paying with cash or plastic, you gave her a Pepsi bottle and said, **"KEEP THE CHANGE."**

Your mother is so stupid, she thought Craig Mack & Biggie Smalls were Value Meals.

Your mother is so stupid, I asked her, "What do you think of the Simpson case?" and she said, "I don't think Bart killed anyone."

Your mother is so stupid, she thought Michael Jordan worked at **DUNKIN' DONUTS.**

Your mother is so stupid, she thought Dr. Jekyll's favorite game was Hyde and seek.

Your girlfriend is so dumb, I said to her, "Are you tan from the Sun?" and she said, "No, I'm Sally from the Earth."

Your mother is so stupid, she has one leg and she's always singing, "Ain't no half steppin'."

Your mother is so stupid, she cooks with OLD SPICE.

Your mother is so stupid, she thinks Ping-Pong balls are a Chinese venereal disease.

Your mother is so stupid, she thought government was a chewing gum.

Your mother is so stupid, she thought Juicy Fruit was a gay person **WITH DIARRHEA.**

Your mother is so dumb, she put the radio in the oven so she could hear some hot tunes.

Your mother is so stupid, she mixed Krazy Glue in her food so it would stick to her stomach.

You're so stupid, you **PICKED YOURSELF** out of a lineup.

You're so stupid, you used Wite-Out on your computer screen.

Your mother is so stupid, she thought Dr Pepper was a seasoning.

Your mother is so dumb, she saw a piano and told it, "Wipe that smile off your face."

Your father is so stupid, he holds a sign saying WILL EAT FOR FOOD.

Your mother is so stupid, she got arrested for stealing donuts because they said Fat Free.

IF BRAINS WERE BACON, you'd be Sizzlean.

Your mother is so dumb, she went to Piccadilly Circus to see the elephants.

Your father is so dumb, he put the clock under his desk so he could WORK OVERTIME.

Your mother is so stupid, she bought a token to get on *Soul Train*.

Your brother is so stupid, I asked him if he was gay and he said, "NO, BUT MY BOYFRIEND IS."

Your sister is so stupid, she went to a travel agent to buy *Jet* magazine.

YOUR SISTER IS
SO STUPID,
SHE HAS ONLY AND
ONE THING SHE
CAN'T
ON HER MIND EVEN
REMEMBER
THAT.

Your mother is so dumb, she dipped you in cement and told you to **THINK HARD.**

Your mother is so stupid, I asked her what state she was born in and she said the state of shock.

Your sister is so stupid, she failed **A TASTE TEST.**

Your mother is so stupid, she tried to answer her calling card.

Your mother is so stupid, she told me she's a tutor because she stands next to the trains and goes **TOOT-TOOT.**

Your sister is so stupid, she thought TLC was a sandwich at Subways.

Your sister is so stupid, I told her my mother is a mute and she said, "Oh, she's down with the X-Men."

Your mother is so stupid, she thought a salary cap was something **SHE WORE ON HER HEAD.**

Your mother is so stupid, she thinks the NAACP is a rap group.

Your mother is so stupid, she thought a sandwich was a wicked lady who lived at the beach.

YOUR MOTHER IS SO STUPID, WHEN I SAW HER JUMPING UP AND DOWN AND ASKED WHY, SHE SAID, "I TOOK SOME MEDICINE AND FORGOT TO SHAKE THE BOTTLE."

UGLY

SNAPS

Your mother is so ugly, **SHE NEEDS A PASSPORT** to go to the beauty parlor.

Your mother is so ugly, they use her at the zoo to stop the monkeys from jerking off.

Your mother is so ugly, her shadow quit.

You're so ugly, the last time you got a piece of ass was when your hand slipped through **THE TOILET PAPER.**

Your parents are so ugly, when they met it was love at first fright.

YOU'RE SO UGLY, WHEN YOU WERE A CHILD EVEN YOUR IMAGINARY FRIENDS WOULDN'T PLAY WITH YOU.

Your mother is so ugly, the doctor looked at her ass and her face and said, "My God, Siamese twins."

Your mother is so ugly, she couldn't get laid in a prison with **A FISTFUL OF PARDONS.**

Your mother is so ugly, when she entered an ugly contest they said, "Sorry, no professionals."

Your mother is so ugly, they moved Halloween to her birthday.

Your mother is so ugly, her **NICKNAME** is Count Chocula.

Your mother is so ugly, she's got hair on her chest going all the way down to her dick.

Your father's so ugly, he wears a knife wound as a part in his hair.

Your sister is so ugly, if she were a stripper they'd yell, "**DAMN, GIRL, PUT IT ON!**"

If ugliness were water, your mother would be Niagara Falls.

You're so ugly, the last time I saw something like you it was walking on a leash.

Your mother is so ugly, they framed her picture with a toilet seat.

You're so ugly, your dog has you ON A LEASH.

Your family is so ugly, when they go to the zoo they show members-only cards.

Your mother is so ugly, I called her a dog and she bit me.

You were such an ugly baby, the doctor THREW YOU AGAINST THE CEILING and told your father, "If it doesn't come back, it's a bat."

Your mother is so ugly, when she goes to the beauty parlor they ask her if she wants paper or plastic.

You're so ugly, when you were born they threw you away and kept **THE AFTERBIRTH.**

Your mother is so ugly, she made a field of onions cry.

Your mother is so ugly, your father takes her to work so he doesn't have to **KISS HER GOOD-BYE.**

If ugliness were toilet paper, your mother would be ten-ply.

YOU'RE **SO UGLY,** **THE ONLY** WAY **YOU COULD GET LAID** IS BY CRAWLING UP A BIRD'S **ASS** **AND WAIT- ING.**

Your mother is so ugly, at Christmas they hang her and kiss the mistletoe.

Your sister is so ugly, she went to a dog show and won.

Your brother is so ugly, when he was born your mother breast-fed him **THROUGH A STRAW.**

Your mother is so ugly, the doctor is still smacking her.

You're so ugly, you went outside and got charged with indecent exposure.

Your mother is so ugly, she makes my hand **GO SOFT**.

Your mother is so ugly, every time she goes outside the sun hides behind the clouds.

Your mother is so ugly, she doesn't look in the mirror because she keeps getting glass in her eye.

Your mother is so ugly, Rice Krispies won't talk to her.

Your sister is so ugly, the only makeup that could help her is **VANISHING CREAM**.

Your mother is so ugly, she looked in the mirror and her reflection ducked.

You're so ugly, when you were born the doctors were fined FOR HAVING AN ANIMAL in the building.

You're so ugly, you had to pay a hooker extra to open her eyes during a blow job.

BIG
AND
SMALL
SNAPS

Your father's dick is so small, he wears a contact lens for a condom.

Your mother's ass is so big, **SHE WORKS AS THE SCREEN** for the drive-in.

Your father's dick is so small, before sex he needs a map that says, "You are here."

Your dick is so small, you lost it in your pubic hair.

Your mother's ass is so big, when she sits down she bounces right back up.

Your sister has one big titty and one small titty, so they call her Biggie Small.

YOUR HEAD IS SO BIG, it takes you three years to lick a head cold.

Your butt is so big, they call you ass fault.

Your mother's tits are so big, kids play Double Dutch with them.

Your dick is so small, it looks like a **MUSHROOM IN A FUR FOREST.**

YOUR NOSE IS SO BIG, YOU CAN PICK IT WITH BOXING GLOVES.

Your butt is so big, when toilets see you coming they put OUT OF ORDER signs on themselves.

Your nose is so big, your boogers look like green apples.

Your father's ears are so big, when he goes to a restaurant people hang their coats on them.

Your mother's chest is so big, SHE HAS TO LOCK HER BRA with The Club.

Your mother's ass is so big, she rents it out as a bus stop.

Your dick is so small, when you have phone sex it keeps getting caught ON THE NUMBER 9.

Your ears are so big, if they hooked you up to a TV you would get cable.

Your ass is so big, you get shit stains on your COLLAR.

HAIR

SNAPS

Your mother's legs are so hairy, when she wears shorts people ask,
"CAN I PET YOUR DOG?"

Your father's hair is so nappy, Moses couldn't part it.

Your mother's legs are so hairy, she wears them in corn rows.

Your mother is so hairy, she has to wash her back with the
MIRACLE PET GLOVE.

Your mother has so much hair on her ass, when she bends over it
looks like Don King.

Your mother is so hairy, she has to part the hair on her wrists to tell what time it is.

Your mother is so hairy, **SHE COULD LIE ON THE PORCH** and be a welcome mat.

Your mother's pussy is so hairy, it looks like the crabs have extensions.

Your sister is so hairy, when she went to the beauty parlor she told the stylist to cut her hair, so he opened her shirt.

Your mother is so hairy, she shaves with a Weedwacker.

Your mother is so hairy, she wears a Nike tag on her weave, so everybody calls her Hair Jordan.

Your mother says she's pretty and young, but she's old as dirt and got hair on her tongue.

Your mother is so bald, you can see what's on her mind.

Your girl's pussy is so hairy, it says WELCOME TO JUNGLE WORLD.

Your mother's hair has more static than a shortwave radio.

YOUR MOM'S LEGS ARE SO HAIRY, **SHE SHAVES** THEM WHEN SHE NEEDS A FUR COAT.

Your brother is so hairy, people call him Nabisco because the hair on his back looks like Shredded Wheat.

Your nappy hair **IS LIKE THE POLICE**—it just rolls up and parks anywhere.

You're so bald, your hairline is like a Just Ice record—goin' way back.

Your hair is like a Chia Pet—short, green, and nappy.

Your boyfriend is so hairy, after you sleep with him you wake up **WITH FLEAS.**

SMELLY

SNAPS

Your sister's breath is so bad, she makes money on the side **PEELING PAINT.**

Your sister's breath is so bad, her pillow took out a restraining order.

Your girlfriend's breath is so bad, her lipstick plays **HIDE-AND-SEEK** in her pocketbook.

Your sister is so stank, we had to put her outside to keep the flies out.

Your breath smells so bad, your tongue's on a stretcher.

Your girlfriend's pussy is so stank, it was condemned by the **BOARD OF HEALTH.**

Your mother's breath is so funky, when she talks her teeth duck.

Your father is so stank, every time he takes a shit they have to put crime-scene tape on the toilet.

Your breath smells so bad, you need a Colgate sandwich.

Your mother is so stank, when she holds her farts it makes her breath **SMELL LIKE SHIT.**

Your breath is so funky, you don't need to carry Mace.

Your mother's breath is so bad, it smells like she's got a little man in her mouth with SHIT ON HIS SHOES.

HOUSE
SNAPS

Your house is so small, it came in a **MONOPOLY GAME.**

Your apartment is like a poker game: It's a full house, the toilets don't flush, and your brothers are a pair of queens.

Your house is so cold, roaches ride around on ice skates.

Your house is so small, when I asked to use the bathroom your mother said, **"PICK A CORNER."**

There are no bathrooms or soap in your house because your family is trying to be filthy rich.

YOUR HOUSE IS SO LITTLE, YOU HAVE TO PUT **YOUR ADDRESS** NEXT DOOR.

YOUR HOUSE IS SO COLD, in the winter you can drink water and shit ice cubes.

Your house is so small, there's no room to complain.

Your house is built out of toilet paper, 'cause your whole family is **FULL OF SHIT!**

Your house is so small, you have to label the dog shit so people don't mistake it for the living room.

OLD
SNAPS

Your mother is so old, she was the first in her family to walk erect.

Your father is so old, he creaks when he walks.

Your father is so old, he has to put his dick **IN THE FREEZER** to get hard.

Your mother is so old, she doesn't have milk in her tits—she has sour cream.

Your mother is so old, when she walks her knuckles drag along the ground.

Your mother is so old, she has a tattoo on her ass saying, "George Washington Slept Here."

Your mother is so old, she knew Big Bird **WHEN HE WAS TWEETY.**

Your mother is so old, she farts mummy dust.

Your mother is so old, her birth certificate says "Expired."

Your grandmother is so old, she remembers getting mad at Adam and telling him to **FIX HIS OWN DAMN SUPPER.**

Your father is so old, when he was a kid rainbows were in black and white.

Your mother is so old, SHE USED TO GANG BANG with the Flintstones.

Your mother is so old, you can see her wrinkles through her blouse.

Your shoes are so old, they've got less soul than Vanilla Ice.

YOUR MOTHER IS SO OLD, she was the first mate on Noah's Ark.

YOUR **MOTHER** IS **SO OLD,** HER TOOTH-BRUSH WAS **A ROCK.**

Your mother is so old, when David killed Goliath she ran to **GET THE COPS.**

Your mother is so old, she gave dancing lessons to the Indians.

Your mother is so old, her Bible is autographed by the author.

Your mother is so old, when God said, **"LET THERE BE LIGHT,"** she struck a match.

Your mother is so old, when she was born they didn't have birth certificates, so they just put her name in the back of the Bible.

POOR
SNAPS

You're so poor, they ask for ID even when you pay cash.

Your family is so poor, your mother's **PERFUME IS GLADE.**

You're so poor, I went into your house, flushed the toilet, and your mother screamed, "What happened to the punchbowl?"

You're so poor, you put free samples on layaway.

Your family is so poor, when you found two boxes you said, "Now I have a **TWO-STORY HOUSE!**"

Your family is so poor, I asked where the bathroom was and your mother said, "Fifth bucket on the right."

You're so poor, when I went to hang up a picture on your wall the nail went straight through the cardboard and into the street.

Your brother is so poor, **HE HAS TO PULL HIS TEETH** for bookmarks.

You're so poor, bums give you money.

Your father is so poor, he shaves with a broken Thunderbird bottle.

Your family was so poor, **YOU GOT SCHOOLING** eating alphabet soup.

Your family is so poor, your dog begs the roaches for scraps.

You're so poor, I came into your house, dropped a cigarette, and the roaches came out clappin' their hands and stompin' their feet, singing, "Thank the Lord we got heat."

You're so country, the stop signs in your 'hood say **WHOOOAH.**

FAMILY IS THEY GO CHURCH HEAT.

Your mother is so poor, her portrait is a court sketch.

Your mother is so poor, **SHE BLEW SANTA CLAUS** for extra batteries.

Your family was so poor, you slept on the bedroom door with Batman sheets.

Your family was so poor, your mother thought the Wheel of Fortune was when your brother got run over by a truck.

Your family is so poor, they give rat traps for Christmas.

Your family is so poor, they use a laundromat as a mailing address.

Your family is so poor that **WHEN SOMEONE TAKES A SHIT** the kids fight to lick the bowl.

NASTY
SNAPS

Your mother's pussy is so big, it's got a diamond lane.

Your sister is so horny, when I told her it was time to eat she opened up her legs.

Your mother's pussy is so big, Boyz II Men sing in it JUST FOR THE ECHO.

Your sister is so loose, Easy Street was named after her.

Your mother is so loose, on FATHER'S DAY you send out fifteen cards.

Your mother's pussy is so big, tourists throw in pennies and **MAKE A WISH.**

Your mother is like an algebra book—she's got a lot of problems, is easy to open, and hard to figure out.

Your mother's pussy is so big, the crabs live in duplexes.

Your mother's pussy is **SO ROUGH**, she uses sandpaper for a tampon.

Your sister is so horny, her vibrator runs on a Die Hard.

Your sister is so horny, when the rooster said, "Cock-a-doodle-do!" she said, **"ANY COCK WILL DO!"**

Your mother is so nasty, she could have been a baseball pitcher, but she let everybody get a hit.

Your feet are so nasty, you have to take your socks off with turpentine.

Your father is so nasty, he can get **RING AROUND THE COLLAR** with a tank top.

Your mother is so nasty, she washes her ass with tartar-control soap.

Your mother is so nasty, when she goes swimming fish follow her.

Your mother is so nasty, there's a sign by her pussy that says **COME AGAIN.**

Your mother is so nasty, I pulled a big fat green one out of my nose and she said, "Wait until it ripens."

You're so nasty, every time you **GO SWIMMING** Exxon has to clean up the spill.

If it wasn't for your chin, I would have no place to rest my balls.

YOUR SISTER IS SO NASTY, SHE EATS PEANUT BUTTER AND K-Y JELLY SANDWICHES.

Your father is so nasty, when you asked what's for dinner he opened up his legs and said, "Sausage and hard-boiled eggs."

Your mother's pussy is so crusty, she sounds like cereal—snap, crackle, and pop.

Your father is on **A SEAFOOD DIET**, 'cause your mother's got crabs on the menu.

Your sister is so nasty, she thinks penicillin is a vitamin.

Your mother is like a cow—she has a snotty nose and dirty tits.

Your mother is so loose, they named a town in New Jersey after her—Freehold.

Your mother is so nasty, when she **TAKES OFF HER KOTEX** it sounds like Velcro.

Your mother is so nasty, she picks her nose, eats the boogers, and calls it recycling.

Your breath is so nasty, you need to drink a Listerine Big Gulp.

Your mother is so nasty, she has toe jam on **HER FINGERS.**

Your mother is so nasty, she has a sign by her legs that says
FILLING STATION.

Your father is so nasty, when he takes your dog for a walk they both piss on the same hydrant.

Your mother is so nasty, she bathes with flea-and-tick soap.

Your mother is so nasty, she sucks dick just 'cause she's thirsty.

Your mother is so nasty, she has to clean out her asshole **WITH A PLUNGER.**

Your mother is so nasty, her ass reminds me of a new store: There are always long lines for **THE GRAND OPENING** and everything's on sale.

Your house is so nasty, the rats and roaches filed a complaint with the Board of Health.

Your father's so nasty, his favorite snack is **BOOGERS AND BITS.**

SHORT
AND
TALL
SNAPS

Your mother's legs are so short, **WHEN SHE WALKS** she leaves a slimy trail.

Your mother is so short, she pole vaults with a toothpick.

You're so short, you need a ladder to kiss a snake's ass.

Your father is so tall, your mother has to stand on the chimney to **GIVE HIM HEAD.**

Your brother is so short and hairy, when he walks around the house your mother screams, "Mouse!"

Your mother is so short, **SHE CAN SWAN DIVE** off a midget's dick.

Your sister is so short, she has to stand up to go down.

Your mother is so short, **SHE HAS TO STAND** on her tiptoes to kiss my ass.

You're so short, you show up when ants have picnics.

Your sister is so short, **SHE USES A COMPACT** for a full-length mirror.

YOUR FATHER IS SO SHORT, HE BOUGHT AN ANT FARM FOR A SECOND HOME.

Your mother is so short, she has to roll down her pants to spit.

Your mother is so short, **SHE CAN GET LOST** in a shag rug.

Your sister is so short, she has to hem her shoes.

Your brother is so short, he has to shower in the sink.

Your brother is so short, he couldn't **HI-FIVE A SMURF.**

TEETH
AND
MOUTH
SNAPS

Your mother's lips are so long, she can **SUCK AN ANT'S DICK** from fifty feet.

Your mother's teeth are so yellow, they look like Corn Pops.

Your brother's so bucktoothed, he can eat his girl without opening his mouth.

Your mother's lips are so big, she can kiss her **OWN ASS.**

Your teeth are so green, when you walk through an intersection the cars run you over.

Your lips are so big, when you went snorkeling a blowfish tried to mate with you.

Your mother's lips are so big, instead of using Chap Stick she uses **MOP & GLO.**

Your lips are so big, you can stand in Brooklyn and be slurping a shake in the Bronx.

You drool so much, you never **NEED TO SHOWER.**

YOUR TEETH ARE POACHERS FOR THE

SISTER'S SO BIG, CHASE HER IVORY.

Your mother's lips are so big, they look like a catcher's mitt.

Your sister has three teeth, one in her mouth and the two in her pussy that the guy left last night.

Your mother's lips are so long, **SHE CAME TO MY HOUSE** to unclog the toilet.

Your mother's teeth are so long, she can kiss you and comb your hair at the same time.

Your lips are like jellyfish—I get seasick every time I see them.

You have **SO MUCH FILM** on your teeth, I thought you were a photographer.

Your teeth are so green, you don't go to the dentist—you go to the Lawn Doctor.

SKINNY
SNAPS

Your mother is so skinny, when she went to the hospital they sent the X ray home and kept her ass.

You're so skinny, **IF YOU STUCK YOUR TONGUE OUT** you'd look like a zipper.

You're so skinny, you can stand under a clothesline to keep out of the rain.

Your brother is so skinny, he breaks into cars without using tools.

Your girl is so skinny, her shadow weighs more than she does.

Your sister's ass **IS SO FLAT,** white women all over the world are jealous.

Your girlfriend's butt is so bony, when she puts on her jeans she cuts them in two.

Your sister is so skinny, she has a job as a cardboard cutout.

Your girl is so skinny, you have to **RUB HER BACK** to play with her nipples.

You're so skinny, if you turn sideways it looks like you left the room.

Your sister is so skinny, she has to **TIE HER LEGS IN KNOTS** to keep her underwear on.

Your sister is so skinny, when she farts her belly button comes out her ass.

BODY
SNAPS

Your mother's fingers are so long, when she picks her nose **SHE TICKLES HER BRAIN.**

Your mother ain't got no fingers, talkin' about she wants to point things out to me.

Your mother is so hunchbacked, **SHE HAS TO WEAR GOGGLES** to take a piss.

Your father's feet are so nasty, they have more crust than Pizza Hut.

Your mother has so many chins, it looks like a stairway up to her face.

Your sister's missing **AN ARM AND A LEG**, but she's still the one for me.

They say your mother has an hourglass shape—the bottom half.

Your mother is blind and she works for Eyewitness News.

Your mother has got knobs on her ass **SO EVERYBODY CAN GET A TURN.**

Your parents have only one eye each and they still can't see eye to eye.

YOU'RE SO CROSS-EYED, YOU SIT ON YOUR FRONT PORCH AND COUNT THE CHICKENS IN THE BACK.

Your mother's so rough, **SHE CAN EAT IRON** and shit BMWs.

Your mother is so cross-eyed, she can watch a tennis match without moving her head.

Your sister is so cross-eyed, if she wants to blow her boyfriend she has to aim at the dick **NEXT TO HIS.**

COLOR
SNAPS

YOUR MOTHER IS SO BLACK, she sets off smoke alarms.

Your mother is so black, her butt looks like a set of tires.

Your mother is so white, moths follow her around.

You're so white, you thought the Black Panther party was an animal rights group.

Your mother is so white, **WHEN SHE OPENS HER MOUTH** kids dunk cookies inside.

Your brother is so black, when he smiles he looks like a domino.

Your girlfriend is so white, if I put her **IN A GLASS** she'd be spoiled milk.

Your mother is so black, if you put your foot in her ass she'd look like a patent-leather boot.

Your sister is so black, **IF HER PUSSY WAS WHITE** she'd look like a Devil Dog.

Your father is so black, he could lie on the ground and be a hole.

YOUR MOTHER IS SO BLACK, SHE COULD SHOW UP AT A FUNERAL NAKED.

Your father is so black, if I crushed him he'd be pepper.

You're so black, **WHEN YOU SHOWER** your Ivory soap turns ebony.

Your mother is so black, she can't even brown-nose.

Your mother is so white, if she put on a cap she'd look like a milk bottle.

Your girl is so white, when she lies on the beach she looks like a slice of bread with two pennies.

Your mother is so white, your sister threw her in the wash along with the rest of the laundry.

You and your sister are so black, if you shared a sleeping bag you'd look like a Twix bar.

You're so ashy, you need to drink a baby-oil Slurpee.

You're so black, **WHEN I FOUGHT YOU** I thought I was shadowboxing.

You're so black, you could use your finger as a pencil.

Your mother is so white, WHEN SHE HAS THE RUNS she shits mashed potatoes.

Your mother is so black, she sweats Pennzoil.

You're so white, when you're eating a carrot you look like a snowman.

SEX
SNAPS

Your mother is so loose, after sex she asks, "Are you boys all on the same team?"

I could've been your daddy, but the guy **IN FRONT OF ME** had correct change.

Your mom is like an A train, $1.50 a ride.

Your mother is like an elephant in bed, 'cause I fuck her for peanuts.

Your sister is so loose, the **FIRST THING** she usually does in the morning is go home.

Your mother is so horny, she drives a car just to use the stick shift.

Your girl is like a Twinkie—always pumped full of cream.

Your mother's like a hardware store— TEN CENTS A SCREW.

Your mother is so loose, if sperm were the fountain of youth she'd live forever.

You're so horny, the last time you got pussy was when you brought a cat home from the animal shelter.

Your mother is like a bubble-gum machine—five cents a blow.

Your mother is like railroad tracks—she's laid around the world.

Your mother has so many cocks going into her, I had to double-park on her ass for an hour.

If dick-sucking WERE A BUSINESS, your sister would be in the Fortune 500.

Your mother keeps her legs open so long, the only place she can shop is at The Gap.

Your mother's idea of world peace is giving everybody on the planet **SOME ASS.**

Your mom is like McDonald's—what you want is what you get.

Your mother is so loose, she coughs sperm.

Your mother is like a vacuum cleaner—she sucks, she blows, and she gets laid in the closet.

Your sister is such a great ball player, **SHE PLAYS WITH MY BALLS** every chance she gets.

Your mother goes out with twelve guys named Richard, 'cause she really likes dick.

YOUR GIRL IS SO LOOSE, she has two-for-one dollar days.

Your mother is like a chicken, always bobbing her head.

I could have been your father, but the line was too long.

Your mother is like the **ENERGIZER BUNNY**—she keeps blowing, and blowing, and blowing

YOUR SISTER IS AFTER SEX WITH HER YOU DON'T SO NASTY, SMOKE A CIGARETTE, YOU GET A RABIES SHOT.

139

Your mother is so loose, her idea of going on a diet is **NOT SWALLOWING.**

Your mother is so loose, when she went to the doctor about a rash on her chin he advised cupping men's balls with both hands.

Your sister is so loose, her lips always look like a glazed donut.

If sperm cleared up skin, your mother would be a Cover Girl.

Your mother is so loose, detectives subpoenaed her teeth and gums **FOR HAIR SAMPLES.**

Your mother is so easy, she's like a Timex watch—takes a dicking and keeps on licking.

Your mother is so loose, she sticks more **NUTS IN HER MOUTH** than a squirrel before winter.

Your mother is so loose, she's like subway tracks—she's under everything that moves and is laid all over the city.

Your mother is like a hair dryer—turn her on and she blows.

Your father is a tri-sexual—name any kind of sex and he's tried it.

Your sister is so loose, when I asked her if she ever did sixty-nine she said, "No. I did seventy once, but I made them all wear condoms."

Just because your brother got caught taking meat in the back, that don't make him a butcher.

Your mother is like a cake—everyone gets a piece.

Your sister is so loose, she sucks dick just to keep her neck from **GETTING STIFF.**

Your mother is like Betsy Ross—she married a Minute Man.

Your mother is like Reese's peanut butter cup—there's no wrong way to eat her.

Your father is so gay, when he went missing they put his picture on the back of the **K-Y JELLY BOX.**

Your mother is so horny, her vibrator comes with dual airbags.

Your sister is so loose, she applied for a job in the night deposit box at the sperm bank.

Your sister's pussy is so big, **IT HAS AN ECHO.**

Your mother is so loose, after sex she turns on the lights by opening the car door.

YOUR FATHER IS SO HORNY, he asked, "How was it for you?" and his partner said, "Moo."

MASTER
SNAPPERS

BY KWAKU
ALSTON

THE AMAZING ADVENTURES OF THE
DARK SNAPPER

145

ACKNOWLEDGMENTS

OUR THANKS TO SOME EXCELLENT SNAPPERS FROM ACROSS THE COUNTRY WHO SENT IN THEIR FAVORITE SNAPS FOR US TO INCLUDE IN THIS BOOK:

MICHAEL ADAMS
Bremen, IN

NICK ADELL
Madison, WI

KEKAILANI AIU
Honolulu, HI

RICHARD ALONSO
Kennewick, WA

BILL ALSTON
Binghamton, NY

ROBERT AMBROZE
Pasadena, CA

ROY F. ATIZADO
Seattle, WA

LINDA AZEVEDO
White Plains, NY

SHAWN BANASAN
Dover, DE

ALFREDO BANUELOS
Modesto, CA

RICK BECKER
Stow, MA

ALFRED BEDONIA
Delano, CA

SARAH BELFORD
Montrose, MI

MATT BELLGRAPH
Binghamton, NY

TONY BERRY
Brighton, England

PETE BEUTTELL
Titusville, FL

DAVID BIRD
Manteca, CA

DOUG BLACK
Birmingham, AL

LUCAS A. BOHN
Matthews, VA

JUSTIN BORUCKI
Chicago, IL

JASON BOSCHERT
APO, AE

KAREN BROWN
Oceanside, CA

BRIAN BURGHOUT
Glendale, AZ

KARLA BURGUENO
Fresno, CA

JOHN CAPRARO
Utica, NY

BECKY CHARITON
Concord, MA

BRIAN CHIN
Flushing, NY

JON CHING
Kapaa, HI

JACOB COLBATH
San Diego, CA

ROBERT COLLINS
Brooklyn, NY

JOY COLTER
Rock Hill, SC

BEN CONNELLY
Fort Wayne, IN

CHRIS CONTAOI
San Bernardino, CA

ANTHONY CONTI
Bayside, NY

JOSEPH CONTRENAS
Covina, CA

JEFFREY COOPER
Rochester, NY

ROSE "BAMBAM" COOPER
Lansing, MI

BOBBY CORD
Clinton, MD

CHARLES CRIPPEN-PROPHET
Philadelphia, PA

RON CUNNINGHAM
Peru, IN

ANDREW CURRIE
Des Moines, IA

DANIEL DEIS
Marina, CA

JASON DIXIE
Fort Wayne, IN

MARCOS DOMICIANO
Union, NJ

MATT DORMAN
Las Vegas, NV

CURT DUELL
Scottsdale, AZ

KURT R. DUGGINS
Stillwater, OK

CHIP DU PONT
Fisher's Island, NY

CHRISTOPHER ECK
Worcester, MA

STEPHAN EGBERT
Orland Park, IL

BRANDON ELLIOTT
Virginia Beach, VA

VINNIE ESPARZA
Oakland, CA

LADONNA ETHERIDGE
Detroit, MI

GEORGE FETTER
Tampa, FL

RONNIE FLORENTE
Visalia, CA

HENRY F. FRANKE, JR.
Waiden, NY

LA KESHA FRAZIER
Reno, NV

SAM GAGLIANO
Rochester, NY

GIOVANNI GALLUZZO
Stamford, CT

ANDY GAMEZ
Blythe, CA

AARON GARCIA
McAllen, TX

CHRISTOPHER GARCIA
Hammond, IN

JILLIAN ASHLEY GELD
Elkins Park, PA

MICHAEL GLICK
Scarsdale, NY

149

MATT GOODWIN
Ardsley, NY

JOE GRAZER
Allentown, PA

DAVE GREENFIELD
New York, NY

BRADLEY GROVER
Winchester, NH

MEGHAN A.
HAFEMAN
Pembine, WI

IAN HALL
Weston, WV

GEOFFREY HARLEY
Chicago, IL

MIKE HASS
Eureka, CA

AARON HAUER
Shelby Township, MI

KEVIN HERALDO
Richmond, VA

IAN HERMAN
Staten Island, NY

CHRIS B. HILL
Hartsdale, NY

DEREK HIRONS
Fiskdale, MA

LESLIE HITTEL
Brockton, MA

NATALIE HOBSON
Richmond, TX

DALLAS LEE HOLGUIN
Venice, CA

LAVALLE HOUSER
Dallas, TX

SHERRY HOWARD
Blakely, GA

ELLIOT JOHNSON
Winneetha, IL

CHRIS JONES
Portage, MI

JASON M.
KAUMANS
Belmond, IA

TODD KEYES
New Orleans, LA

WARREN KLARMAN, JR.
Inverness, FL

KENTON KOGA
Pearl City, HI

GLENN KROLL
Great Neck, NY

BRIAN KUHN
Grand Junction, CO

JOE LAM
Collings Lakes, NJ

JIM LARSEN
Greenville, OH

MICHAEL AND
JORDAN LEFF
Bedford, NY

MORRIE H. LEW
Rolling Hills, CA

JAMES LITTLEJOHN
Texarkana, TX

TIM LOEBBAKA
Mt. Prospect, IL

TONY LOO
Seattle, WA

RENANN LOPEZ
Daly City, CA

ANTWAIN LOVE
Chicago, IL

KRISTA LOWE
Hooper, UT

RAY LUGO
New York, NY

CHRIS LUMPKIN
San Diego, LA

JOHNNY MA
San Jose, CA

RODERICK
MACUGAY
Lihue Kauai, HI

BETHANY MACNEUR
Beaverton, OR

SCOTT MADDUX
Albuquerque, NM

NICK MANJARREZ
Wapato, WA

JOSH MARTIN
Cedar Rapids, IA

JESSE MASON
Cape Girardeau, MO

RHONDA MATHEWS
Milledgeville, GA

BUBBA MAYS
Aviston, IL

ALVIN L.
MCCARVER III
Chicago, IL

JONATHAN
MCGRAW
Bloomfield Hills, MI

MICHELLE MCKINNON
Las Vegas, NV

MAC MCMURRAY
Lake Worth, FL

ADAM MEAGHER
Revere, MA

MANNY MEDINA
North Haven, CT

MELISSA MEGAS
Albany, NY

JILL MENECKER
Bayside, NY

ROBERT
MENNONNA
Rocky Point, NY

DERRICK
MILENKOFF
Hobart, IN

BERNY MITCHELL
Philadelphia, PA

KIYOMI MIZUKAMI
FPO, AP 96349

LILLIAN K. MOLLER
Los Angeles, CA

SEAN MONAHAN
Mililani, HI

ALEXIS MONTOYA
Woodland, CA

LORI MOONEY
Bronx, NY

DEREK
MUCKELROY
Kilgore, TX

SEBASTIAN
MURESAN
Modesto, CA

MATTHEW MURPHY
Kirkland, WA

MYLA
The Netherlands

DAVID MYRICK
Monterey, CA

BRAD NACIO
Gretna, LA

DANIEL NADOLSKI
New Britain, CT

TYLER NORBY
Portland, OR

JEFF OBAYASHI
San Diego, CA

JON OH
Torrance, CA

CHRISTOPHER
MIGUEL OLIVARES
Oakland, CA

SHARRIEFF OMAR
Germantown, MD

DEREK ORCHARD
Reno, NV

JESSIE ORTIZ
Wapato, WA

NATALIE M.
PADILLA
Santa Barbara, CA

LONNIE PARKER
Dunbar, WV

ALMAR PASCUA
Santa Clara, CA

MARK PASCUA
Daly City, CA

MARY PASCUA
Daly City, CA

KEVIN PAUL
Burbank, CA

HOLMES POOSER
Reno, NV

RANDY PORTER
Belmont, MA

KIM POWELL
Kankakee, IL

SKOT PRUCKER
NMB, FL

DANNY PUENTE
San Antonio, TX

MICHAEL RAGASA
Wailuku, Maui, HI

MATTHEW RAY
Harrisburg, PA

TARA J. RAY
Fontana, CA

BECKY REUSS
Pierce, NE

GARY R.
REYNOLDS, JR.
Atlanta, GA

DAVID RICHARD
Clarksburg, WV

DEBBIE ROAQUIN
Glendale, NY

MORGAN ROCKEY
Maple Valley, WA

ANNIE ROMO
Santa Barbara, CA

CIANE RUSSELL
Roanoke, VA

ANGELLA
SAAVEDRA
Queens, NY

LOUIS ST. LEWIS
Chapel Hill, NC

JENNIFER SALINAS
White Plains, NY

DAVID SALING
New Orleans, LA

KAARON SAPHIR
New York, NY

DEREK SAUNDERS
Evansville, IN

KATIE SCHAFFER
North Tonawanda, NY

COVAR SEARS
Bethleham, PA

KEN "LIZARD"
SHEIDE
Okinawa City, Japan

PETER SIDLOVSKY
Farmington, CT

KIMBERLY SILVA
Keaau, HI

DONALD SMILEY
Charlotte, NC

KIMBERLINE SMITH
Hawthorne, CA

RICHARD C.
STANGE
Philadelphia, PA

NATHAN STEVEN
Dubuque, IA

MASULAH SURMATY
Burke, VA

DAN SWEET
Kingston, RI

BRIAN SZAFRANSKI
Port St. Joe, FL

CHRISTINA
TALIAFERROW
Brooklyn, NY

ALEX TAMAYO
El Centro, CA

CHRIS TOBIA
New Haven, CT

JUSTIN TODD
Memphis, TN

STEVEN TONG
Alameda, CA

JOHNATHAN
TORRES
New York, NY

LYDIA TOTH
Sunnyvale, CA

PAUL TRAN
Sterling, VA

KIM TROUPE
Topeka, KA

BRIAN TYLER
Shelbyville, KY

UNKNOWN
Antelope, CA

FRANKLIN
VASQUEZ
Daly City, CA

ANDREA
VELAZQUEZ
Staten Island, NY

DRUERVONN L.
WASHINGTON
Detroit, MI

CHARLES R. WELCH
Charlotte, NC

AARON WERMAN
Atlantic Beach, NY

STEVEN WESSOCK
Erwinna, PA

LINDY WHEATLEY
Champaign, IL

JAMES WHEELER
Hailey, ID

MICHAEL
WILBEKIN
Bronx, NY

DAVE WILSON
Crown Point, IN

LISA YOUNT
El Cerrito, CA

JOSEPH YRULEGUI
Fresno, CA

WILLIAM ZARATE
Lynwood, CA

Aileen Argentini • Bill Bellamy • Jack Benson • Rip Beyman • Richard Blumenthal • Linda Burke • Irene Cara • Johnnie Cochran • George Carlin • Dave Chapelle • Neil Cogan • Gleynice Coleman • Coolio • Larry Dais • Dr. Dre • Ashante Douglas • Tina Douglas • Jay Durgan • Abe Dweck • Mildred Dweck • Hafiz Farid • Gangstar • Mayor Rudy Giuliani • Tina Graham • Guru • Ricky Harris • Austin Hearst • Heavy D • Bruce Hill • Jorge Hinojosa • Ice-T • Claude Ismael • Jack the Rapper • La Mama Experimental Theatre Club • Lawrence Hilton Jacobs • Homer Jolly • Hettie Jones • Kelly Jones • Lisa Jones • Big Daddy Kane • Craig Kallman • Melisa Katz • Mitchell Klipper • Andrew Leary • David J. Leiter • Michael Lewittes • Lords of the Underground • Ed Lover • Bernie Mack • Anthony Malatino • Allen Marchioni • Biz Markie • Brad Marks International • Jim McGee • Bill Miller • Kendall Minter, Esq. • Tea Money • Roger Mosley • Wendy Moten • Andy Nulman • Dana Orlikoff • Glenn Orenstein • Bruce Paisner • Production Partners • Maria Perez • Jon Rubin • Leonard Riggio • Stephen Riggio • Rysher Entertainment • Guy Rouchon • Michael Rudell, Esq. • Keith Samples • Jim Signorelli • Scripps Howard Productions • Roy Smith, Esq. • Alan Sosne • Ellen Stewart • Arnie Stone • Joel Stillerman • Kevin Swain • Chuck Sutton • Bob Tate • Dedra Tate • Jeanine Tate • Carey Thomas • Liz Tzetzo • Suzanne Vega • Merrill Vladimer • Kevin Weaver • Veronica Webb • Alyson Williams • Frank Wolf

AND THANKS TO THOSE WHO CAN SNAP EVEN BETTER THAN WE CAN...

Cheryl Abbott • Sharon Alexander • Joan Allen • Keith Armstrong • Mercedes Ayala • Katisha Baldwin • Baltazar • Bart Bartolomeo • Donna Baynes • Lola Yvonne Bell • Louis Bell • Terrence Benbow • Benny B. • Bentley's • Mike B. • Big L • Big Warren • Black Filmmaker Foundation • Julie Black • Michael Blackson • Eric Boardman • Michael Braver • Brooklyn Mike • Willie Brown • Buckwild • Monica Butler • J. C. Callender • Kelly Campbell • Toni Campbell • Mike "Checka" Caren • Stephanie Carney • Crystal Castro • Bridette Chin • Lisa Clarke • Yvette Coit • Caribbean Cultural Center • Donald Chapman • Ava Cherry • Dave Chappelle • Joe Claire • Chris Cohen • Linda Coles • Diane Corder • Sean Couch • Andre Cousins • Douglas Crew '78 • Kathie Davidson, Esq. • Maria Davis • Pat DeRosa & PDR Productions • Diamond • Diamond D • Charlie Dixon • D.K.

• Albert Dotson, Esq. • Doug E. Doug • Jeanine DuBison • Barry Dufae • Susan Duncan • Dr. Monica Dweck • Natalie Dweck • Vaughn Dweck • Michael Epps • Donald Faison • Figman • Nabi Faison • Shirley Faison • Diana Farmer • Fat Joe • Lord Finesse • Flex • Hope Flood • Harry Fobbs • Scott Folks • Ronda Fowler • Monica Fox • Sundra Franklin • Stewart Friedman • Ardie Fuqua • Diane Gaffney • Dianne Gibbs • Dr. Steven Glickman • David Gallen • Jody Gerber, Esq. • Carole Green, Esq. • Kechin Greene • Rona Greene • "Little Tiny" Heard • Ernie Hill • Jordan Horowitz • Lisa Humphrey • Beverly Ivey • Ollie Ivey • Waverly Ivey • Crystal Jackson • Gloria Jackson • A. J. Johnson • David Johnson • Alonzo "Hamburger" Jones • Jamal Joseph • Sydney Joseph • Poetic Justice • Larry Kahn • Elaine Kaufman • Ada Keibu • William Keller • Gerald Kelly • Barry Kibrick • David King • John Henry Kurtz • Patricia Lawrence • Rodney Lemay • Jerry Levanthal • Don Levin • Rich Lewis • Eric Libird • Michael Libird • Persina Lucas • Macio • Uncle Jimmy Mack • Johnnie Mae • Maija Martinez • Doris McCormick • Doxie Mc Coy • Debbie Miller • Monijae • Monique • The Staff of Monty's Comedy Crib • Corwin Moore • Hugh Moore • Tracy Morgan • Stacy Moseley • Roger Mosley • Patrick Moxey • Mugga • Earl Nash • National Black Theatre • Kenny Nealy • John Noonan • Jim O'Brien, Esq. • Joellyn O'Loughlin • Mark Overton • Sharon Parker • Jim Pasternak • Lawrence Patten • Consuelo Patterson • Debbie Pender • Lew Perlman • Al Pizzaro • Alan Potashnick • Preacher Earl & the Ministry • Dorothy Pringle • Ratzo • Lisa Ray • Ray Ray • Andre Reyes • Andre Richardson • Freddie Ricks • Ray Rivera • Rudy Rush • Jack Sahl • Tracy Salmon • Tunde Samuel • John Sanpietro • Cleo Sanders • Laura Sanders • Neil Schwartz • Dick Scott • Robert and Marsha Seely • Judith Service • Dave Sheppard Showbiz & AG • Joe Siegal • Sheri Sinclair • Rickey Smiley • Miyoshi Smith • J. B. Smooth • Jeri Snead • Somore • Special K • Brian Sroub • Rob Stapleton • Rosalyn Strain • Bob Sumner • Bruce Tabb • Talent • Veronica Taylor • Barbara Ann Teer • Ernest Thomas • Randy Tibbott • Wayman Tisdale • Ana Tolentino • Keith Truesdell • Paul Ungar, Esq. • Michael Vann • Marta Vega • Rich Voz • Michael Walton • Theobald Walton • A. G. White • Marchene White • Doreen Whitten • Michael Williams • Hilda Willis • Ghana Wilson • PaSean Wilson • Richard Winkler • Stanley Winslow

SPECIAL THANKS TO THESE RADIO PERSONALITIES AND NETWORKS WHO HAD THE NERVE TO INTERVIEW US:

ALEX BENNETT SHOW	KITS	San Francisco, CA
ZOO CREW	KMEL-FM	San Francisco, CA
RICK CHASE SHOW	KMEL	San Francisco, CA
MIKE CHASE	KDON	Salinas, CA
DJ NALVER	KWIN-97.7	Stockton, CA
MIKE CHASE	KDON	San Francisco, CA
WILLIS JOHNSON SHOW	KKDA-AM	Dallas, TX
SKIP MURPHY	KKDA-FM	Dallas, TX
DAYTIME MAGAZINE	KKDA-FM	Dallas, TX
COUSIN LENNY	KKDA-AM	Dallas, TX
DON IMUS	WFAN	New York, NY
HOWARD STERN	WXRK	New York, NY
MIKE SEARGENT	WBAI	New York, NY
DAVID BRENNER	Westwood One	New York, NY
MARK RILEY	WLIB	New York, NY
CYNTHIA SMITH	WLIB	New York, NY
THE MIKE WALKER SHOW	Westwood One	New York, NY
DRE & LOVER SHOW	Hot 97.WQHT	New York, NY
LISA G.	Hot 97.WQHT	New York, NY
AARON GOLDMAN	WNYU	New York, NY
MICHELE WRIGHT & BAT JOHNSON	WBLS	New York, NY
TRENT TAYLOR	Q104.3 WAXQ	New York, NY
CHRISTINE NAGY	Q104.3 WAXQ	New York, NY
SALIM MWAKHU	WVON-AM	New York, NY
BIG JOHN TOBIN	101.5 WPDH	Poughkeepsie, NY
THE WOLF	101.5 WPDH	Poughkeepsie, NY
MAD MIKE	101.5 WPDH	Poughkeepsie, NY
BROTHER WEUSE	WZMF-AM	Rochester, NY
BACKSTAGE PRESS	WBEZ (NPR)	Chicago, IL

JOHNNY VOHN	WLS	Chicago, IL
MANCOW	WROX	Chicago, IL
MIKE & CAROL SHOW	WVEE-103 FM	Atlanta, GA
HOT ICE IN THE AFTERNOON	WCLK-FM	Atlanta, GA
MORNING SHOW	WIBB-97.9 FM	Atlanta, GA
BERNIE MCCAIN SHOW	WOL-AM	Washington, DC
JONES & CO.	WMMJ	Washington, DC
LAURENCE GREGORY JONES	WMMS	Washington, DC
DAVE & BRIAN	WUSL-Power 99	Philadelphia, PA
NICK TALIAFERRO	WHAT-AM	Philadelphia, PA
THE WOODY & JEWEL SHOW	WCAQ	Philadelphia, PA
STEVE JOHNSON	WEZB	New Orleans, LA
GARY SPEARS	WEZB	New Orleans, LA
SAM GILES	96.3 WROV	Roanoke, VA
MARK NELSON	96.3 WROV	Roanoke, VA
JEFF OH	96.3 WROV	Roanoke, VA
RICK BARBER SHOW	KOA-AM	Denver, CO
BIG DAVE & THE DUKE	WKDF	Nashville, TN
SCOTT OVERTON	CIGM	Ontario, Canada
STEVENS & GRIDNICK	All-Star Radio	Syndicated

ABOUT THE AUTHORS

2 BROS. & A WHITE GUY, INC., is a production company formed by a producer, a comedian, and an entertainment attorney. The principals authored the best-selling books *Snaps* and *Double Snaps* and introduced the word *snaps* into the lexicon. They have produced a series of *Snaps* TV specials for HBO and a humorous antiviolence image campaign for MTV. The company recently coproduced a *Snaps* CD on Atlantic Records and a *Snaps* CD-ROM . They are currently creating *Snaps: The Movie* for Live Entertainment and developing a sitcom about their unusual company.

JAMES PERCELAY is a writer/producer whose background includes production on the parody commercials for *Saturday Night Live* and documentaries on subjects ranging from The Dance Theatre of Harlem to The Rolling Stones. James is a former head of development at Hearst Entertainment and has produced projects for all three major networks. He is a member of the WGA and is heading up the *Snaps* CD-ROM project and Web site. James was executive producer for the HBO series *Snaps* and will also be executive producer on the upcoming *Snaps* movie.

STEPHAN DWECK is a prominent New York entertainment attorney specializing in music and television. Stephan's clients include over forty recording artists ranging from current top-forty bands on major labels to underground acts, which he cultivates. Stephan represents over seventy-five currently working TV and film actors. He is also counsel for the The National Black Theatre. Stephan teaches a weekly entertainment-law course at Baruch College and was co-executive Producer for the HBO *Snaps* series. He will also be serving as co-executive producer on the *Snaps* movie.

MONTERIA IVEY is a writer/comedian. He is the creator of Monty's Comedy Crib, Harlem's premiere comedy club. Monteria is affiliated with the Black Filmmaker Foundation and hosts their live events. He performs stand-up comedy nationwide, opened HBO's '93, '94, and '95 live Toyota Comedy Festivals, and is currently touring as warm-up comedian for the HBO Comedy Hour. Monteria is represented by the American Program Bureau to lecture at colleges on African-American humor. Monteria was co-executive producer for the HBO *Snaps* TV series and was the show's host. He also hosted twenty-two episodes of the PBS game show *Think Twice,* produced by WGBH, Boston. Monteria stars in the upcoming *Snaps* CD-Rom and will be co-executive producer for the *Snaps* movie.

GET YA SNAPS STUFF

The Shirt
High-quality white T-shirt w/2
Bros. logo on sleeve and funny
two-color snap on front. Plus
official hang tag on sleeve.

The Hat
Black baseball cap w/red
SNAPS logo on front and two-
color 2 Bros. logo on back.
One size fits all.

O R D E R   F O R M

Name ▲

Address   Apt #

City   State   Zip Code

(   )
Phone

Payment by Certified Check, Money Order or:

☐ Mastercard   ☐ Visa   ☐ AmExpress

_____ / /
Account #   Expiration date

Item	Price	Qty	Amount
Hat	$12.98		
T-Shirt (Large)	$14.98		
T-Shirt (X-Large)	$14.98		
Subtotal			
NY residents add 8.25% sales tax			
Shipping			$3.50
Total Due			

Please allow 4 to 6 weeks for delivery.

© **BROS. & A WHITE GUY, INC.**   9 2 6 1 1 - 2
P.O. Box 764, Planetarium Station, New York, NY 10024-0539

We would like your comments on this book,

as well as your favorite original snaps.

If we include your new snaps in our next book,

we'll acknowledge your contributions.

P.O. Box 764

Planetarium Station

New York, N.Y. 10024-0539

@HTTP://WWW.SNAPS.COM